Consumer Smarts
Getting the Most for Your Money

Jeri Freedman

ROSEN
PUBLISHING

New York

Published in 2013 by The Rosen Publishing Group, Inc.
29 East 21st Street, New York, NY 10010

Library of Congress Cataloging-in-Publication Data

Freedman, Jeri.
Consumer smarts: getting the most for your money/Jeri Freedman.
—1st ed.
    p. cm.—(Get smart with your money)
Includes bibliographical references and index.
ISBN 978-1-4488-8254-0 (library binding)—
ISBN 978-1-4488-8260-1 (pbk.)—
ISBN 978-1-4488-8261-8 (6-pack)
1. Consumer education. I. Title.
TX335.F7194 2013
381.3'3—dc23

                                                    2012026583

Manufactured in the United States of America

CPSIA Compliance Information: Batch #W13YA: For further information, contact Rosen Publishing, New York, New York, at
1-800-237-9932.

Contents

ROSEN 1305 23

Shopping with friends is a fun social activity for many people. Making the most of your money can make the experience more enjoyable.

Introduction

For most people, shopping is a necessity. For many people, shopping—at least some types—is fun. However, when shopping you can fall into the trap of spending a lot of money without thinking about the consequences. Learning to shop smart can allow you to buy more of the things you want with the same amount of money. In addition, it can help you save a significant amount of cash that you can use later for a larger purchase, such as a car.

It's easy to fritter money away by paying more for items and services than necessary. Often it seems as if the small amounts of money wasted here and there don't matter, but these small amounts saved regularly can become large amounts of money over time. Save $50 per month for a year, and you'll have $600. Do that for the four years you are in high school, and you'll have $2,400. Do it for twenty years, and you'll have $12,000. Put it in a savings account paying 1 percent interest, and you'll have $14,075.00 at the end of those twenty years. Invest it in a stock mutual fund from a reputable company, and, given the average lifetime 7 percent return of the stock market, it could be as much as $28,640 after twenty years. That's why the time to start thinking about how you use your money is now, while you're young.

More important than the money you save now, however, are the habits that you develop. If you develop good financial habits while you're young, you are likely to continue those habits throughout your life. Shopping smart means more than just buying things cheaply. It means learning to judge the value of the items you are thinking of buying and paying the appropriate amount of money for the features and quality you need. It means learning to estimate the useful life span of items you buy. It also means learning to judge what things you need to buy now and what can wait until later. Because many items can be purchased in a variety of brick-and-mortar and online stores, learning how to find the best place to buy is important— as is learning how to protect yourself when purchasing items.

These principles apply to a wide range of products and services. You can learn how to get the most for your money when buying clothing, consumer electronics, games and books, food, personal care products, and entertainment. Saving money is not a matter of scrimping, but of using money wisely so you have more in the long run. The true nature of thrift is getting good quality for less.

Chapter 1
Shopping for Clothes

Just as important as what you buy is where you buy it. Sometimes when you go shopping for clothes, you are looking for a particular item you need, and sometimes you're just casually browsing with friends or hanging out at the mall. This section covers how to get the best prices for clothing at department stores and chain stores, as well as alternate places to buy clothing for less.

Making the Most of the Mall

When you're cruising the mall with friends, it can be fun to check out the stores. Think of the mall as a directory of items you can purchase from a variety of sources. Before you purchase something, ask yourself whether you can find the same item for less money at a different store or online.

Most stores have sale or clearance racks that they continuously restock. If you are browsing in a department store, browse these racks first. If you find an item there to buy, you're less likely to be tempted by full-price merchandise because you've already had the satisfaction of scoring a find. Make a list of full-price items you see that

Waiting for items to go on sale can help make your money go further. Many expensive items receive large markdowns when space is needed for new merchandise.

you'd like to buy, and then wait for a sale or clearance and go back and buy the item for less.

Practice the thirty-minute rule. When you see something you think you'd like to buy, leave the store—go to the food court, have a soda, chat with your friends. If you find that after thirty minutes you still can't stop thinking about the item, then you probably really want it. If you can't remember what you were looking at, you don't need it.

Brand Names for Less

If you're interested in name-brand clothing, try shopping at overstock stores such as T.J. Maxx and Marshalls. When

Avoid the Status Trap

Learn the difference between style and trendiness. Trendiness means buying the brands and styles that TV commercials, magazines, and online ads tell you to buy. These brands and styles change from year to year. They are promoted by sports stars and pop culture icons, such as singers and actors. The most notable features of these items are that they cost a lot of money in comparison to nontrendy brands or items, and they go out of style very quickly when a new trend comes along.

It's natural to want to look cool. However, a lot of overpriced trendy merchandise is purchased simply out of

Fashion magazines provide advice on how to dress well. Looking good depends on understanding the rules of how to dress, not on how much money you spend on clothing.

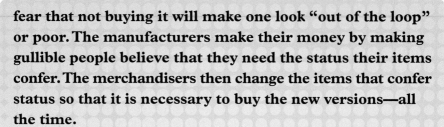

fear that not buying it will make one look "out of the loop" or poor. The manufacturers make their money by making gullible people believe that they need the status their items confer. The merchandisers then change the items that confer status so that it is necessary to buy the new versions—all the time.

Style, in contrast, is flair and fashion sense that make you look attractive or put together. If you learn the rules of style and fashion, you can purchase items that make a positive impression over time instead of wasting your money on items that will no longer be trendy next month. There are many good books and magazines devoted to style and fashion. The advantage of choosing style over trendiness is that it allows you to develop a look that is not only striking but also personal. Be a fashion leader, not a follower. Knowledge about style can help you dress well as you enter the workforce and socialize throughout your life, not just now. So, learn to look good for less.

manufacturers produce items to sell to the department store chains, they have to make a guess about how many of each item to make. If the stores do not buy as many of each item as expected, or if sales at the department stores are slow because of economic factors, the manufacturer is left with unsold merchandise. Similarly, if the department store chains buy too much merchandise, they need to get rid of the excess to make room for the next season's merchandise. All of this excess merchandise is called overstock.

Overstock stores, such as this T.J. Maxx in Washington, D.C., give shoppers the opportunity to buy brand-name merchandise at significantly reduced prices.

Stores such as T.J. Maxx, Marshalls, and Ross buy this excess stock at a large discount, which means that, in turn, they can sell it to customers for less. These are great places to buy department store–quality clothing for much less than the department stores charge. Just remember to check the quality or labels of the items you buy, as well as the price. Overstock stores sometimes supplement their purchases of brand-name items with cheaply made non-brand-name merchandise.

Another source of overstock items is outlet stores. Many manufacturers such as Nike and Reebok, among others, sell their excess merchandise in outlet stores that are either

Avoid the Credit Trap

It's not unusual for teens to have access to credit cards. Sometimes they are cosigners on their parents' cards. Certainly, once you turn eighteen, credit card companies are likely to start peppering you with offers for cards. Companies such as Visa and MasterCard promote their cards as a pain-free alternative to cash. One well-known slogan says, "There are some things money can't buy. For everything else, there's MasterCard."

What the ads don't tell you is that the things you buy with credit cards are not free. The debt you rack up on credit cards can become a burden in owed payments you'll carry for years to come. It is very easy to build up a huge debt with a credit card. The credit card companies charge fees and finance charges for using their cards. The finance charges can be as much as 23 percent of your purchases. These fees are added to the total amount on the card, so the next month's fee is larger if the card is not paid off each month. Every month, you have to pay a certain percentage of the balance, so the monthly payment gets bigger as the balance gets bigger. The money you must pay to the credit card company is money you can't spend on other things.

Therefore, it is best to use credit cards only for emergencies, not for buying things you want but don't have the cash to pay for. If you feel you simply can't live without a pretty blouse or an electronic toy, that's a time for self-discipline. Get the money together in cash, and then buy it. To make life easier, many stores are now offering layaway programs. In these programs, customers put a small amount of money down and then pay a little each week until the item is paid for. Layaway is an excellent way to pay for an item over time without building up debt. If you have a credit card, leave it at home when you go shopping.

stand-alone stores or located in outlet malls with other outlet stores. As with other overstock stores, however, be careful what you purchase. It has become common practice for brand-name manufacturers to stock their outlet stores with regular merchandise that isn't any cheaper than the items at their mall stores or that is made especially for sale at the outlet store. You may need to hunt through the outlet store to find the genuine items at a reduced price. Sometimes it's cheaper to buy such merchandise at regular discount stores.

You also need to consider the price of an item in terms of how long you're likely to use it. If you're buying a coat that you plan to use for several years, it may be smart to pay more for a high-quality item that will wear well for a long time. If you're buying a skirt that's going to be out of style next year, you'll want to buy something less expensive.

Alternative Shopping

For real bargains, try nontraditional shopping venues, such as thrift shops, flea markets, and yard sales. Church or synagogue rummage sales can be good places to find bargains as well. It's amazing how many cool shirts, blouses, jackets, accessories,

TODAY
50% OFF
EVERYTHING
WITH A ➤
PRICE TAG

WHITE

One can often find fun accessories and clothing at thrift shops. Buying and donating clothing at thrift shops allows it to be reused instead of thrown out.

and pieces of jewelry are available at yard sales and rummage sales in good neighborhoods, often in beautiful or even new condition.

Flea markets are another source of inexpensive but attractive clothing. Some of the clothing at flea markets is used, as it is in a thrift shop. Other items are sold by vendors who specialize in overstock items, such as jeans and T-shirts, which they buy in bulk and sell for less than in department stores. When purchasing goods at flea markets, you need to be sure you're getting what you pay for, however. Some flea market and online vendors who claim to be selling brand-name merchandise may, in fact, be selling cheaply made knockoffs. Some of these copies can look good on you, but you want to pay an appropriate price—significantly less than what you'd pay for a higher-quality item.

There are positive side effects of doing some of your shopping in alternate venues. In many instances, money spent at thrift shops or rummage sales goes to charitable organizations, so you are not only saving money but also giving money to a good cause. As a matter of fact, when you have clothing that is in good shape but that you no longer use, don't throw it out. Donate it back to a charity's thrift shop so the shop can sell it again.

Myths & Facts

Myth   The most expensive item is usually the best quality.

Fact   With many expensive brand-name and designer items, you are paying primarily for the advertising and endorsement dollars the companies spend promoting them. Their quality may not be any better than other brands.

Myth   You save the most money by buying the cheapest item.

Fact   Sometimes the cheapest item is poorly made and doesn't last long or work reliably. Therefore, price alone is not the best criterion on which to base a buying decision.

Myth   If I don't buy the expensive items my peers are buying, they'll think I'm a loser.

Fact   When you emerge from college with enough money to buy a car or put a down payment on a place to live, your peers will be jealous—assuming you even still know the people who were popular when you were in high school. Further, since the economic downturn, it has become trendy to use money wisely.

Chapter 2
Shopping for Consumer Goods

There are many different ways to buy fun items—books, movies, music, and electronics—including online ordering and downloading, as well as purchasing them in brick-and-mortar stores.

Electronic devices are among the most popular purchased goods. This category includes MP3 players, TVs, DVD and CD players, gaming consoles, tablet computers, and all of the accessories that go along with these devices. These items often cost a great deal of money, so it is important to make sure you get what you are paying for. Here we'll discuss ways to get electronic goods at the best price, as well as other important issues to consider when buying electronics, including ensuring that a product is good quality, deciding whether to buy product warranties, and weighing the pros and cons of buying online.

Getting the Best Price for Consumer Electronics

There are two major ways to purchase electronic devices, gaming devices, and computers—in

Buying a large number of a few products allows warehouse clubs like Costco to buy electronic items for less than traditional stores can. The clubs then pass the cost savings on to their customers.

brick-and-mortar stores and online. The advantage of purchasing from a store is that you can see and touch the merchandise. You can compare the look of different manufacturers' models and get a feel for how easy or difficult a device is to use. The disadvantage is that physical stores often charge more than online sources because of their overhead expenses, such as rent, electricity, and sales staff.

The advantage of buying online is that prices are often lower than in brick-and-mortar stores. Online merchants can charge less because they do not have to maintain physical premises or pay as many employees. The disadvantage is that you can't see or touch what you are buying, so you have to be certain that you are buying from a trusted source. If you do buy electronics online, it's best to stick to well-known, established companies—otherwise, you could lose your money. If you choose to purchase a device online, be sure to include the shipping costs when estimating what the item will cost you. There's little point in buying a device for $50 less online and then paying a $50 shipping fee. For many items, online vendors offer free shipping, especially on more expensive items.

There are a wide variety of brick-and-mortar stores to choose from, ranging from specialty retailers such as BestBuy to discount stores such as Wal-Mart, Costco, and Sam's Club. Often the discount venues have very low prices, but the setup of the device is left entirely to you. Specialty electronics stores may charge more for a device, but they may also provide services such as setup or installation.

Online sites such as BizRate and Dealtime gather price data on electronic items from a large number of stores, using "bots" (short for robots). The bots search the Web and compile a list of prices from various manufacturers for each item. This allows you to do a side-by-side comparison of what an item costs at different stores and online sources.

Don't forget about sales and coupons. Most stores have both regular and after-holiday sales. After you've decided what you want to buy, it may be worthwhile to check out the weekly circulars from electronics and general retailers in your area to see what's on sale. Also, for many items it's possible to do an online search using a search engine such as Google, Bing, or Yahoo! for "[name of item] coupon" to see if there are any coupons or special offers for the item you wish to buy.

A major factor in the decision about whether to buy online is the type of item you are buying. If you are purchasing a Wii game system, then the product will be the same regardless of where you buy it. If you are buying a stereo entertainment system, you will most likely want to see and try out the various makes and models in person.

If you do buy online, you will need access to a credit card. If your parent pays for the device with his or her credit card, suggest using a card that has a consumer protection feature. This feature allows the buyer to dispute the charge if the device fails to show up or doesn't work. That way your money is not at risk.

Warranties

Most consumer electronic devices come with a manufacturer's warranty. This covers repairs for a specific period of time, such as one year. If you are buying a high-ticket item such as a computer or TV, it is worthwhile to examine the manufacturer's warranty coverage. Check whether the coverage includes both parts and service. Also check if you have to send a broken device back to the manufacturer or if you have the option to bring it to a local service center. ConsumerReports.org recommends skipping the extended warranty protection stores often try to sell you. Most consumer electronic devices last longer than the warranty. If they don't, the cost of replacement is often only a little more than the extended warranty protection. In addition, by the time the device dies, there's usually a new, upgraded model available. Also, it's often more convenient to buy a new item than to send the old one back and live without it while waiting for it to be fixed. Technology changes so quickly today that a long warranty is rarely needed.

Cell Phones and Smartphones

Cell phones and smartphones are a special category of electronic device. Often, if you want a specific phone, such as an iPhone, you are limited to the cell phone service providers that sell and support the brand or model you are interested in. You still have some options when purchasing a phone, however. Some service providers offer a choice of plans with prices that vary for specific services and lengths of time. Which plan you buy may affect how much you pay for a phone. In addition, providers sometimes run specials such as buy one, get one free or buy one and get a second at half price. So be sure to ask about any special promotions when purchasing a phone. Some phones are available from several different providers, in which case, it is worthwhile to compare the prices and promotions at different companies.

Customers wait to purchase iPhones at a Verizon store. Now that several major carriers offer popular iPhone and Android phones, it pays to compare various plans and promotions before purchasing.

Books, Movies, Music, and Games

Some of the best bargains around are available when shopping for books, music, movies, and computer games. There are three major ways of buying these items: purchasing them in a store, ordering online, and downloading them. Many of the same bargain-hunting tips that apply to electronics apply to these items as well, such as looking for sales and coupons. However, there are a few twists.

First, there is the issue of trade-ins. A number of stores such as GameStop and BestBuy sell used as well as new games and will offer credits for used games. There are also a number of Web sites that offer downloads of older games for free or at a minimal cost. If you play games online, avoid wasting real money on "virtual" items. Use your real money to buy real items in the real world.

One of the decisions you need to make when buying books, music, or movies today is the item's format. Do you want a physical copy that you can keep and use more than once? Do you want an electronic version of a book or movie you can read on your smartphone, tablet, or e-reader, such as the Kindle or Nook? Usually, physical copies are the most expensive, and downloads are the least expensive. However, physical copies can be traded or sold when you are done with them, while downloads cannot. Also, downloads may be device- or manufacturer-specific. For example, a book designed to be read on a Kindle, or a Kindle app on your smartphone or computer, may not be usable if you switch to a Nook, and vice versa.

The fact is, a book or DVD is the same regardless of where you buy it. This means that you can shop around for the best price. Sometimes brick-and-mortar stores such as Barnes & Noble offer large discounts on books that are best sellers. Online retailers such as Amazon offer generous discounts on books, CDs, DVDs, and games, especially used copies. If you order online, it's best to batch several items in an order, or make a combined order with friends, to qualify for discounts such as free shipping.

Used bookstores are another source for inexpensive books. Often you can acquire a title for half of the retail price or even less. Many used bookstores also take books as trade-ins for credit toward the purchase of other items. For books you only want to read once, the best bargain is your local library. Taking a book out of the library costs nothing, and you can use your money for other things. If a library branch does not have the book you want, it may be able to get the book from another

At used bookstores you can buy recent books at bargain prices. You can also find out-of-print books on subjects that interest you.

library in its system. Many libraries will also take requests for books and will purchase items that its patrons request.

One of the best bargains for movies is using downloading services such as Netflix. For a small monthly fee, these services allow users to download unlimited movies and TV shows. The services are usable on a wide range of devices, including digital TVs, smartphones, tablets, and computers. The advantage of using a service like Netflix is that it offers a huge number of movies and TV shows. The cost for download-only service is inexpensive, and you can use it on all the different devices you may own. One disadvantage is that the latest movies are not always available in downloadable format, and there is an additional charge to have physical discs sent. Also, using the service with a television requires purchasing a device such as a Blu-ray player, Wii, or adapter. More players are entering the online movie download market, however, which should provide a wider variety of options and prices for users.

Alternative Shopping

There are numerous alternative ways to buy items such as books, CDs, DVDs, and computer games for a very small outlay of cash. One can often find media items at yard sales, flea markets, and rummage sales. Recent items are available online from auction sites such as eBay and Amazon's Marketplace, often for only a few dollars plus shipping. Be sure to check the feedback on the seller. If you have any doubts about whether an item is an original or a copy, e-mail the seller directly and ask if it's the original commercial version. If you don't receive an answer, don't trust the dealer.

The nature of electronics sold on online auction sites varies. Some are overstock items bought in bulk by dealers who then sell them online at much lower prices than retail stores offer.

Knockoffs, Counterfeits, and Piracy

In flea markets and online venues, as well as some over-stock stores, there are often items that look like their brand-name counterparts but are actually imitations. Knockoffs are goods that are made to look like popular brands but are usually lower-quality items made of cheaper materials. For example, a vendor at a flea market may sell watches that resemble popular brands at very low prices. If they resemble the item in question, but have small variances, they are merely cheap imitations. Such items may even be a good deal because, although they're not well made, they don't cost much. If you're going to get bored with the trend in a few months, then quality and durability don't matter.

On the other hand, if the knockoff items sport the trademarks of the brands they imitate, they are counterfeits, which are illegal. A major problem arises when expensive electronic items appear to be real but are actually counter-feits. These items will probably not work as well or for as long as their legal counterparts will. One giveaway on such items is price. If the price of an electronic device seems absurdly low compared to what it sells for in stores, then be wary: it might be a counterfeit.

A special form of counterfeiting is piracy. This involves making and selling illegal copies of software, music CDs, DVDs, or computer games. Such items often don't work well—or at all. In addition, in the case of soft-ware, they might contain viruses that can infect your

Use care and common sense when buying goods from street dealers. Knockoff watches, purses, CDs, and videos may be counterfeit or pirated.

computer. When purchasing items in venues such as flea markets, it's relatively easy to see if an item's packaging looks like the original. However, when buying online from auction sites and small dealers, it's not as easy to tell. So, be sure to ask whether a dealer is selling the original commercial version of the product with the original packaging.

These items are often new and come with manufacturers' warranties. However, overstock items may be older versions of a product, and spare parts may not continue to be available for them. Other items on auction sites are used. While they may be in good working condition, it is wise to buy from sources that offer protection for buyers in case the products don't work. Other electronic items may be refurbished. These are items that are used or were returned to the manufacturer because of a problem. The dealer has fixed, or refurbished, the item and is now offering it for sale. Honest dealers will indicate that their items are refurbished. This can be an inexpensive way to get certain items, and if the dealer is a shop, such as "Big Al's Camera Shop," it may even provide a warranty for the product.

Library book sales are another excellent source of both recent and older books, as well as DVDs and CDs. Libraries in many towns hold book sales on an annual or more frequent basis. These sales help raise money for the library and often have hundreds or even thousands of books with prices of only a dollar or two. If you're not sure if the library in your town holds a book sale, check with the librarians there or do an online search for "Friends of [name of town] Library book sale." An excellent source for book sales is the Web site Book Sale Finder (http://booksalefinder.com), which provides a large list of book sales divided by state and month.

Online Comparisons and Reviews

When you purchase an electronic device, there are three major issues: cost, features, and quality. Regardless of whether you make your purchase in a brick-and-mortar store or online, it's important to do your homework before you buy. This way, you can ensure you are getting the right item at the right price.

You can find reviews of many items in popular electronics, media, and computer magazines. These reviews often provide an in-depth description of the features of the device and explain what the experience of using it is like. Such magazines are often available online as well as in print.

The Web is an excellent tool for researching price and quality. There are two main types of review sites on the Web: expert and personal opinion. Expert sites are those like ConsumerReports.org. The organization that publishes the site tests items in different categories for a wide range of features and performance issues. Then reviewers write a report rating each product's quality. The findings are based on expert analysis, not just personal opinion. The Web site charges a subscription fee, but it is an invaluable resource when buying expensive items.

There are many sites on which consumers can provide feedback about their experiences with a product. Amazon, BizRate, and Yahoo! Shopping are just a few. In addition to posting user reviews, these sites often compile a product rating (such as one to five stars) based on people's feedback. The value of these sites is the ability to gain an overall impression of the model or product you are interested in. If the reviews seem consistently positive or negative, that is important information. The individual user's experience may or may not be the same as yours because people have different expectations and needs. However, if you wish to get an answer to a specific question, such as "Is the device easy to use?" or "Is it reliable?" you might find an answer by reading individual consumer reviews.

Ten Great Questions to Ask
A MERCHANT

1 Is this item compatible or usable with other items I own? (Give examples.)

2 Is this item likely to go on sale? When?

3 Is the store offering any special promotions or discounts?

4 Is a newer model coming out soon?

5 Does this store offer a rewards or loyalty card?

6 Where was this item made or imported from?

7 Do you sell a similar product with more (or fewer) features?

8 Does this item have a manufacturer's warranty, and how long does it last?

9 If there is a problem with the product, can it be repaired at the store or a local service center, or does it have to be shipped back to the manufacturer?

10 How long do I have to return this item? Will I receive cash or store credit?

Chapter 3

Shopping for Food, Medicine, and Personal Care Products

W e all need food, personal care products, and, sooner or later, medicine. Even with these necessities of life, there are ways to save money.

Saving on Basics

Sometimes when people shop for basic necessities, they want to purchase a brand-name product. People often have fierce loyalty to their favorite brands of cookies, toothpaste, shampoo, and other products. However, the prices for brand-name food and personal care products may vary considerably depending on where they are purchased. The most expensive places to buy personal care products and cosmetics are department stores. The second-most expensive venue is the grocery store—and for food, it is the drugstore. Grocery stores buy large amounts of food products and small amounts of "drugstore" items such as shampoo; drugstores do the reverse. Manufacturers charge retailers less per item if a product is purchased in large quantities. Therefore, food usually costs more at drugstores, and personal care items usually cost more at

Dollar stores, such as this Family Dollar store in Memphis, Tennessee, are becoming an increasingly popular venue for price-conscious shoppers.

grocery stores. Buying products at the appropriate retailer is the first step in getting the most for your money.

In recent years, different types of chain stores have developed that buy products in even larger quantities than groceries and drugstores. Because of the volume of items these companies sell at their extensive networks of stores, their prices on both food and personal care products can be significantly lower than those at groceries and drugstores.

Discount retailers include stores like Target and Wal-Mart. These stores offer a limited number of branded items but buy them in huge quantity. As a result, cost per item is lower than that of traditional groceries and drugstores. If the store carries the brand you want, the price is often much lower. In addition to low cost, discount retailers offer the advantage of carrying a wide range of product types, so you can pick up personal care products, food, and household goods all at the same time. The disadvantage is that they often carry only a few major brands, so you may not be able to buy every item you need or want there.

"Dollar stores" have also become very popular, especially since the economic downturn. Some examples are the Dollar Store, Family Dollar, and Dollar General. Everything in these stores may not be exactly a dollar, but their prices are very low compared to the prices for the same products elsewhere. They carry personal care products, food, school supplies, and often other items such as DVDs, books, games, and general household products. They are an excellent source of cheap items for school, entertainment, and household use. However, when purchasing food or items such as toothpaste, which you put in your body, some caution is advisable. Some of the items sold in these stores are made in foreign locations, such as China, where quality is not as rigorously controlled as in the United

BJ's Wholesale Club is an example of a membership warehouse. In return for an annual fee, club members get significant savings on products sold in bulk.

States and Canada. There have been instances in which con-
tamination was found in such products. Unfortunately, this can
be the case even with brand-name products, which have on
occasion turned out to be counterfeit. If you have any doubts
about the source or quality of a product, check with the manager or err on the side of caution and purchase it elsewhere.
Also, remember to check expiration dates. You want to make
sure that the product hasn't been sitting on the shelf or in a
warehouse for so long that its "use-by" date has passed.

A third type of store that sells inexpensive personal care
items is the overstock store. Overstock stores include Big Lots,
Ocean State Job Lot, and Building 19. These retailers buy
excess inventory from manufacturers at huge discounts and
pass the savings along to consumers. The advantage of overstock stores is that the products are often very cheap. The
disadvantage is that the quality of some products can be poor,
and there is no telling what they will have in stock at any time.
Overstock stores are great places to browse and get bargains
but hard places to fill a shopping list.

Finally, there are the warehouse clubs. These are chain
stores like Costco, Sam's Club, and BJ's Wholesale Club. These
stores sell items in bulk or wholesale quantities to consumers.
For instance, they sell food by the case instead of small, individual boxes, and cosmetics in very large bottles. Their prices
are often significantly lower than those of traditional grocery
stores or drugstores for the same items. In addition to food
and personal care products, they are a great source for other
necessities, such as school supplies and batteries in bulk. They
are a fabulous place to shop if you need a large amount of
food or supplies for a school or social event. The disadvantage
of warehouse clubs is that they charge an annual membership
fee, and they offer only a limited choice of brands.

The Online Alternative

Online retailers such as Amazon.com, HarmonDiscount.com, and Drugstore.com offer a variety of food, household, pet, and personal care products. These products are sold to the customer directly or through partner companies. Often one can buy products in individual units or by the case for less than in brick-and-mortar stores. It is possible to go to such a site, type the product you are looking for into a search box, and see what your options are. In some cases, shipping may be free, but in other cases there may be charges, so consider that cost as well when purchasing online.

The online option is particularly useful when you are looking for a food or personal care product that is difficult to find in your area. The online approach is most appropriate for personal care, household, or pet items that are not subject to spoilage. There is no way to check the quality of online food items, as there is in person, so when purchasing food items online, be sure to check out the return or refund policy of the vendor. As always when purchasing online goods, be sure to use a credit card that provides protection in case of a dispute with the vendor.

Make the Most of Coupons

Regardless of which type of store you choose to shop in, look for coupons for the food and personal items you buy, both in print and online. Also check out the weekly circulars from stores in your area. Stores often advertise "loss leaders." These are items offered at very low prices, on which the store may not make any profit. They offer these bargains to get customers into the store. As long as you stick to the bargains, you can save a lot of money. One caution about coupons: use them to

Today, it's possible to download product coupons instantly to a smartphone. The coupons contain bar codes that allow them to be scanned right at the checkout counter.

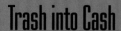

Trash into Cash

One great way to buy stuff you want is to sell stuff you don't want. Are you planning to clean out your closet, basement, or other storage areas where you've shoved toys, games, clothes, sports equipment, and other items that once interested you, but that you no longer use? Collect all of these items. With the help of your parents, hold a yard sale or sell them on eBay. You'll be surprised at how much extra cash you can raise. An added advantage: your parents may thank you for clearing out a lot of the family's "junk." To make the effort more fun, enlist your friends in the project. Have them do the same thing, and hold a group sale.

buy things you usually buy. Don't be fooled into buying things you normally don't buy simply because they're a bargain—in that case, they're not.

Major drugstores and department stores periodically have sales or coupons for 20 or 30 percent off your entire purchase for one or two days. If you know of a store that does this, it may pay to make a list of things you want to buy and wait for such a sale. In many stores, customers can sign up for free reward cards to receive coupons in the store or via mail or e-mail.

Buying Brand Name vs. Generic

There are two basic types of products: brand name and generic. Brand-name products are proprietary to the company that

By not paying for fancy packaging, manufacturers save money on generic products. Companies pass this savings on to consumers.

makes them. Such products are protected by trademark or patent for a certain number of years after a company develops them. During this period, the company has the exclusive right to manufacture and sell the product. After this period expires, other companies can make copies of the product. These non-brand-name versions of the product are called generic products. There are two types of generic products: general and store brand (sometimes called "private label" or "store's own"). Some generic products are sold under the manufacturer or distributor's brand. These products, like their brand-name counterparts, are sold in different stores around the country. Store brands are made for a particular store and carry a name unique to that store, such as Wal-Mart's Great Value line of food.

Using generic products can provide great savings. However, as with brand-name products, the quality of generic products can vary. Therefore, you may find you prefer one generic brand to another. At one time, the same companies that made the brand-name products also manufactured the generic brands. Therefore, you could count on getting the same quality that you would with the brand name. The cost was lower because the store selling the product didn't have to cover the advertising and packaging costs that the brand-name company did. This is no longer true in many cases. Many of the companies that make generic products today specialize in making generic products. Therefore, you may find that in some cases, generic products contain less "product." There may be less of the active ingredient in the detergent, or less vegetable and more liquid in the can. In other cases, the product may be just as good, or even better, than the name-brand versions. For this reason, it may be necessary to try different generic versions of a product to find one that suits you. Also, when comparing prices, make sure that the generic and brand-name packages contain the same amount of the product or are the same weight. It's no bargain to pay 20 percent less for a box that weighs 20 percent less.

This is especially necessary to be aware of when purchasing over-the-counter health and personal comfort products. Be sure to look at the active ingredients lists on the labels. While in many cases the amount of active ingredient is the same, sometimes the generic costs less because there is less of the active ingredient in the product.

One further caution is advisable when purchasing over-the-counter generic medications, such as allergy pills. Although, by law, the active ingredients must be the same in brand-name and generic versions of medications, the inactive ingredients do not have to be the same. The inactive ingredients used for binding, for example, can affect how easily the active ingredient in a pill is released or how quickly a coating on the pill dissolves. In most cases, generic medications work as well as their brand-name counterparts. However, if a generic medication does not seem to be working as well, trying a different generic or returning to the brand-name version may be in order.

CHAPTER 4
Shopping for Entertainment

There are many amazing bargains one can take advantage of when it comes to entertainment such as movies, plays, concerts, and sporting events. Some types of discounts are offered to the general public. Many additional discounts are available only to students. Being familiar with these options can save you a lot of money.

Visit It for Less

There are a vast number of museums, historical sites, and natural attractions around the country. The full-price admission to these venues can be expensive, but many offer students a discounted rate. In addition, there are even less expensive ways to take advantage of these attractions. The cheapest way to see an attraction is for free. Many schools, clubs, libraries, and even companies such as banks have free passes to sites that members can borrow. If you do borrow such a pass, be sure to return it in a timely fashion so others can use it. Also, many museums have one evening a week when they are free to the public.

It's common for local amusement parks and tourist attractions to offer discounts at times when attendance is low. You can often find such coupons online and at local retailers.

Coupons are another great way to save money on entertainment. These come in both paper and online varieties. Local businesses such as convenience stores and doughnut shops sometimes get stacks of coupons offering discounts for area amusement parks or for seasonal events such as carnivals and haunted houses. Before you visit an attraction, check out its Web site. It's not unusual for local and seasonal attractions to

Travel for Less

A number of Web sites offer discounted rates on travel, including hotels, rental cars, and airline flights. Two examples are Hotwire and Priceline. These sites can offer lower rates because they are filling rooms or seats that the vendors have calculated will go unused. Unlike consumer goods, which can be sold the next day or the next week, travel services that aren't sold on a particular day are gone forever—and so is the revenue associated with them. Therefore, the vendor would rather get something than lose 100 percent of the value of the service. One option such sites sometimes offer is "name your own price." With this option, buyers offer to pay what they want for, say, a hotel room in a specific city. The system tries to find a hotel that will accept the offer. If it succeeds, the buyer is committed to accepting that reservation. If the offer price is too low, the buyer will be told the minimum a vendor will accept. The advantage of this approach is that a person can get travel services very cheaply. The disadvantage is

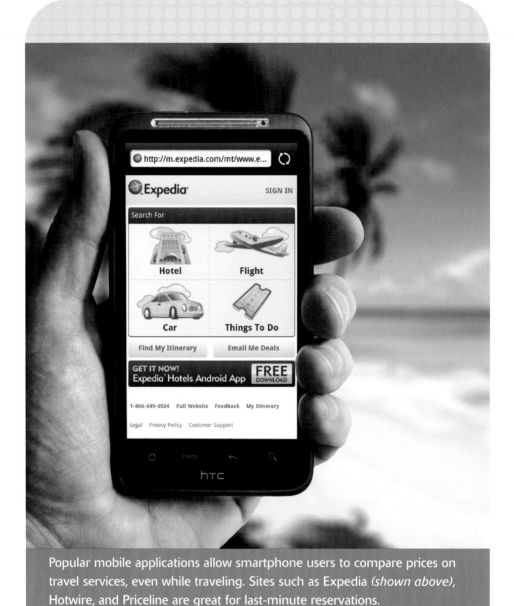

Popular mobile applications allow smartphone users to compare prices on travel services, even while traveling. Sites such as Expedia *(shown above)*, Hotwire, and Priceline are great for last-minute reservations.

that there is no choice about what type of room you'll get or exactly which vendor will accept the offer. Even for those who don't want to name their own price, these sites can be an excellent source for highly discounted services.

A second type of online travel site functions by finding all the service providers who meet a user's criteria for travel. Examples of this type of site include Travelocity and Expedia. With these sites, a user inputs the dates of travel and the location where he or she wants to go. The site searches a database of hotels, airlines, and the like. It then provides the user with a list showing the various travel options and their prices. This can be a great tool. It allows the customer to see at a glance what prices various vendors are offering, so one can choose the best option. It also lets the customer see if adjusting the schedule slightly would result in a large reduction in price. Such travel sites also offer discounted travel packages that can save customers money compared to what it would cost to purchase a number of different services separately.

post a coupon on the Web that you can print and take with you. Many Web sites for major attractions such as Universal Studios and Disney World allow you to sign up for special offers. These often include discounts if you visit off-season and sometimes even free admission on your birthday. Many national attractions provide discount coupons you can access by visiting their Facebook pages.

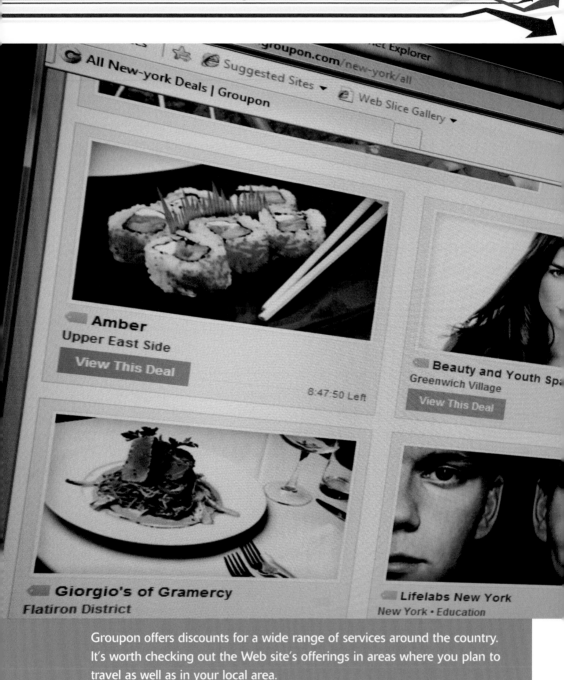

Groupon offers discounts for a wide range of services around the country. It's worth checking out the Web site's offerings in areas where you plan to travel as well as in your local area.

Kew Gardens Cinemas
Kew Gardens

View This Deal

NYC Adventure Boot Camp for
Central Park - Upper East Side

Coupon books, such as *The Entertainment Coupon Book,* are sold for major cities around the country. These books offer two-for-one meals and discount tickets for attractions. Such books can be purchased online as well as locally in bookshops and other stores. To make a coupon book worthwhile to buy, you must use several of the coupons, but since the book is relatively inexpensive, you can save a lot of money if you eat out often with friends. Also, check out your local yellow pages. Many now have several pages of discount coupons for local businesses, including restaurants.

Another way to save money on attractions and events is to sign up with a service such as Groupon or Valpak. These companies provide discount offers on restaurant meals, attractions, services, or products in a specific city. Buyers must purchase the offers in advance, but they can save as much as 50 percent.

If you haven't got a coupon, you still may be able to get a discounted ticket if you or your parents belong to an auto club such as AAA. These clubs often sell discounted tickets that you can use for admission to attractions. Stop by your auto club's local office, or check online for a list of attractions for which it offers such

Going to the movies at times when tickets are cheapest can save you money, as can joining a cinema's rewards club.

tickets. In addition, local attractions often have package tickets that allow you to visit a number of attractions in a city for a price significantly lower than the cost of all of the individual tickets combined. Such tickets are typically available at any one of the attractions included, so when visiting an attraction, ask if they offer any combo tickets with other attractions in the area.

See It for Less

There are a number of ways to save money on movies. On days when you are not in school, try going to the movies during the day, when theaters have trouble filling their seats; you can get tickets at significantly reduced prices. Another way is to buy tickets in batches from membership warehouse clubs, which offer multipacks of tickets for major cinema chains at discount prices. If you see a lot of movies, or want to split the price with your friends, you can save money this way. Just be sure to read any restrictions regarding when the tickets can be used. Also note that a number of theater chains are now offering reward cards to keep customers coming back. These cards may provide discounts on tickets and/or reduced prices on concessions like popcorn and soda.

Many theaters and sporting and concert venues offer free or highly discounted tickets at the last minute to shows that are not full or that feature new talent, in order to fill seats. Contact your local theaters and arenas to see if they have sign-up lists or offer special student discounts. Another way to see a play or event for free is to volunteer. Events often rely on volunteers for a variety of tasks such as setup, ushering, and cleanup. In return, you get to see the show for free. Keep an eye out for local festivals that are scheduled to occur in your area. Some of these offer free entertainment. Others need volunteers.

Use It for Less

The cheapest type of entertainment is also the healthiest. Exercise can help keep people from becoming obese and developing certain diseases, such as diabetes, which are becoming far too common among young people. Physical activity performed at a young age has beneficial effects over a lifetime, but some workouts can be boring. Hiking, swimming, canoeing, biking, and other outdoor activities can be engaging forms of exercise. Such activities help you to stay in shape while spending time in an attractive environment. Most areas have state parks where people can engage in such activities for free. On a federal level, national parks combine a venue for challenging outdoor activities with natural wonders that are worth seeing. The national parks periodically feature "free days," especially around holidays. In addition, they often use volunteers.

If you enjoy a sport such as skiing or horseback riding, and there are facilities near where you live, check out opportunities to volunteer or work part-time or seasonal jobs. These jobs usually allow you to use the facilities when you are not working.

As you can see, there are many ways to save money on the things you like to do and buy. Remember, getting the most for your money now gives you more to use in the future.

Glossary

bots Software that searches sites on the Internet to capture information.

brick-and-mortar store A physical store that people shop at in person.

confer To give to someone.

consumer electronics Electronic devices purchased by people for personal use.

consumer goods Products purchased by individuals rather than by businesses.

criterion A standard on which a decision or judgment may be based.

generic A non-brand-name version of a product.

icon A recognizable symbol or person whose image has come to represent a field.

inventory The quantity of goods or items in stock.

knockoff An imitation or copy of a brand-name or popular product that sells for less than the original.

layaway A program in which a customer makes a small down payment and regular payments for an item and receives the item when it is paid off.

merchant The manager of a retail business; storekeeper.

outlet store A store at which a company sells its excess inventory at a reduced price.

overhead The expenses that a business incurs in carrying out its activities, such as electricity, rent, and salaries.

overstock Excess inventory.

overstock store A store that purchases excess inventory from manufacturers or full-price chain stores and sells it at discounted prices.

patron One who buys the goods or uses the services offered by an establishment.

personal care items Over-the-counter products people use to improve their looks or health.

pop culture Products and activities that reflect the taste of the general public.

proprietary Unique to and controlled solely by a particular company.

refurbished Repaired and returned to usable condition.

retailer A store that sells in small quantities directly to the consumer.

thrift Wisdom and caution in the management of money.

thrift shop A shop that sells used clothing and other goods and is often run by a charity.

use-by date A date stamped on a product that indicates when it expires.

vendor One that sells; seller.

venue The location at which an activity occurs.

warranty A statement guaranteeing the good condition of a product for a certain period of time and stating the manufacturer's responsibility for the repair or replacement of faulty parts.

wholesale The sale of goods in large quantity, usually for resale by a store or other business.

For More Information

American Association of Family & Consumer Sciences (AAFCS)
400 N. Columbus Street
Suite 202
Alexandria, VA 22314
(703) 706-4600
(800) 424-8080
Web site: http://www.aafcs.org
The AAFCS provides leadership and support for professionals
and students in the field of family and consumer
sciences. Members assist individuals, families, and
communities in making informed decisions about their
well-being, relationships, and resources to achieve
optimal quality of life.

Canadian Council of Better Business Bureaus
St. Clair Avenue East, Suite 800
Toronto, ON M4T 2T5
Canada
(416) 644-4936
Web site: http://www.bbb.org/canada/consumers
The Canadian Council of Better Business Bureaus advises the
Council of Better Business Bureaus on important issues
relating to businesses and consumers in Canada.
Consumers can check out businesses in Canada through
this organization.

Consumers Union
101 Truman Avenue
Yonkers, NY 10703-1057
(914) 378-2000

Web site: http://www.consumersunion.org

This organization is "an expert, independent, nonprofit organization whose mission is to work for a fair, just, and safe marketplace for all consumers and to empower consumers to protect themselves." It publishes *Consumer Reports* magazine.

Council of Better Business Bureaus
3033 Wilson Boulevard, Suite 600
Arlington, VA 22201
(703) 276-0100
Web site: http://www.bbb.org/us

This organization provides information to consumers about businesses and charities. Consumers can use its resources to check out a business before buying its products or services or to check out a charity before donating money to it. The organization also provides information about consumer scams.

Family, Career and Community Leaders of America (FCCLA)
1910 Association Drive
Reston, VA 20191
(703) 476-4900
(800) 234-4425
Web site: http://www.fcclainc.org

The FCCLA is a nonprofit national career and technical student organization for young men and women in family and consumer sciences education through grade twelve. The organization helps members expand their leadership potential and address important personal, family, work, and societal issues through family and consumer sciences education.

Federal Trade Commission, Bureau of Consumer Protection
600 Pennsylvania Avenue NW
Washington, DC 20580
(202) 326-2222
Web site: http://www.ftc.gov/bcp
The FTC's Bureau of Consumer Protection works to protect
consumers against unfair, deceptive, or fraudulent practices
in the marketplace. It conducts investigations, sues companies and people who violate the law, develops rules to
protect consumers, and educates consumers and businesses
about their rights and responsibilities. You can submit
complaints about consumer fraud or identity theft online
or by phone.

Office of Consumer Affairs (OCA)
Industry Canada
C. D. Howe Building
235 Queen Street
Ottawa, ON K1A 0H5
Canada
(613) 954-5031
(800) 328-6189 (Canada only)
Web site: http://www.ic.gc.ca/eic/site/oca-bc.nsf/eng/home
This organization addresses consumer issues in Canada. Its
Web site provides a Canadian consumer handbook and a
guide to building one's buying skills.

U.S. Consumer Product Safety Commission (CPSC)
4330 East West Highway
Bethesda, MD 20814
(301) 504-7923
(800) 638-2772

Web site: http://www.cpsc.gov
This agency is charged with protecting the public from unsafe
    products that can cause injury or death. It tests products
    and provides information on recalled products and
    product safety.

Web Sites

Due to the changing nature of Internet links, Rosen Publishing
has developed an online list of Web sites related to the subject
of this book. This site is updated regularly. Please use this link
to access the list:

http://www.rosenlinks.com/GSM/Cons

For Further Reading

Bellenir, Karen. *Cash and Credit Information for Teens* (Teen Finance). 2nd ed. Detroit, MI: Omnigraphics, 2009.

Brancato, Robin F. *Money: Getting It, Using It, and Avoiding the Traps: The Ultimate Teen Guide* (It Happened to Me). Lanham, MD: Scarecrow Press, 2007.

Chatzky, Jean Sherman. *Not Your Parents' Money Book: Making, Saving, and Spending Your Own Money.* New York, NY: Simon & Schuster Books for Young Readers, 2010.

Donovan, Sandra. *Budgeting Smarts: How to Set Goals, Save Money, Spend Wisely, and More* (*USA TODAY* Teen Wise Guides: Time, Money, and Relationships). Minneapolis, MN: Twenty-First Century Books, 2012.

Hamm, Trent. *365 Ways to Live Cheap: Your Everyday Guide to Saving Money.* Avon, MA: Adams Media, 2009.

Hansen, Mark Victor. *The Richest Kids in America: How They Earn It, How They Spend It, How You Can, Too.* Newport Beach, CA: Hansen House, 2009.

Kirk, Ellen. *Human Footprint: Everything You Will Eat, Use, Wear, Buy, and Throw Out in Your Lifetime* (National Geographic Kids). Washington, DC: National Geographic, 2010.

Lawrence, Lane, and Tom Ridgway. *Buying Goods and Services* (Dollars and Sense: A Guide to Financial Literacy). New York, NY: Rosen Central, 2011.

Mandell, Lewis, and Cobblestone Publishing Company. *It's Just Money: The Science of Spending.* Peterborough, NH: Cobblestone Publishing Company, 2010.

Rockliff, Mara. *Get Real.* Philadelphia, PA: Running Press, 2010.

Samtur, Susan J., and Adam R. Samtur. *Supershop Like the Coupon Queen: How to Save 50% or More Every Time You Shop.* New York, NY: Berkley Books, 2010.

Scheff, Anna. *Shopping Smarts: How to Choose Wisely, Find Bargains, Spot Swindles, and More* (*USA TODAY* Teen Wise Guides: Time, Money, and Relationships). Minneapolis, MN: Twenty-First Century Books, 2012.

Silver, Don. *High School Money Book*. Los Angeles, CA: Adams-Hall Publishing, 2007.

Spencer, Kathy, and Samantha Rose. *How to Shop for Free: Shopping Secrets for Smart Women Who Love to Get Something for Nothing*. Cambridge, MA: Da Capo Life Long, 2010.

Vickers, Rebecca. *101 Ways to Be Smart About Money* (101). Chicago, IL: Raintree, 2012.

Watkins, Heidi. *Consumer Culture* (Issues That Concern You). Detroit, MI: Greenhaven Press, 2011.

Wilmes, Karen. *The Everything Couponing Book: Clip Your Way to Incredible Savings!* Avon, MA: Adams Media, 2012.

Bibliography

Angles, Paul. "1001 Best Ways to Save Money." 1001 BestWays. com, 2011. Retrieved March 2, 2012 (http:// www.1001bestways.com/category/save_money).

BeingFrugal.net. "101 Ways to Cut Your Spending This Year." January 6, 2010. Retrieved March 1, 2012 (http:// beingfrugal.net/2010/01/06/101-ways-to-save-money).

ConsumerReports.org. "Buying Electronics, Get the Best Price." November 2007. Retrieved February 28, 2012 (http:// www.consumerreports.org/cro/electronics-computers/ resource-center/where-to-buy-electronics-11-07/get-the-best-price/buying-electronics-get-the-best-price.htm).

FinancialHighway.com. "45 Ways to Save Money." Retrieved February 27, 2012 (http://financialhighway.com/45-ways-to-save-money).

FrugallyMinded.com. "How to Save Money on Entertainment. Retrieved March 6, 2012 (http://www.frugallyminded.com/ entertainment/how-to-save-money-on-entertainment).

GoodHousekeeping.com. "25 Easy Ways to Save Money in 2010." Retrieved March 1, 2012 (http://www.goodhousekeeping. com/family/budget/save-more-money).

Ingram, Leah. *Suddenly Frugal: How to Live Happier & Healthier for Less.* Avon, MA: Adams Media, 2010.

McCoy, Jonni. *Miserly Moms: Living Well on Less in a Tough Economy*. 4th ed. Minneapolis, MN: Bethany House, 2009.

MoneyAside.com. "10 Tips to Save Money on Household Items." Retrieved February 28, 2012 (http://www .moneyaside.com/10-tips-to-save-money-on-household-items).

101 Ways to Save Money. "Save on Entertainment." Retrieved March 6, 2012 (http://www.101waystosavemoney.com/Save-On-Entertainment.html).

101 Ways to Save Money. "Save on Household Items." Retrieved February 28, 2012 (http://www.101waystosavemoney.com/Save-On-Household-Items.html).

Popken, Ben. "43 Ways to Save Money." Consumerist.com, February 24, 2011. Retrieved February 27, 2012 (http://consumerist.com/2011/02/44-ways-to-save-money.html).

RecessionHacks.com. "How to Save Money on Household Items in a Recession." Retrieved February 28, 2012 (http://www.recessionhacks.com/frugal-living/save-money-household-items).

The Simple Dollar. "Little Steps: 100 Great Tips for Saving Money for Those Just Getting Started." February 6, 2008. Retrieved March 1, 2012 (http://www.thesimpledollar.com/2008/02/06/little-steps-100-great-tips-for-saving-money-for-those-just-getting-started).

Slide, Casey. "How to Save Money on Groceries: The Top 20 Ways to Save." MoneyCrashers.com, December 9, 2011. Retrieved March 2, 2012 (http://www.moneycrashers.com/ways-save-money-groceries).

Turner, Jo. "101 Ways to Save Money." Alabama Cooperative Extension System. Retrieved March 1, 2012 (http://www.aces.edu/pubs/docs/H/HE-0562/HE-0562.pdf).

U.S. News & World Report. "5 Ways to Trim Your Grocery Bills." MSN Money, October 5, 2011. Retrieved February 27, 2012 (http://money.msn.com/shopping-deals/5-ways-to-trim-your-grocery-bills.aspx).

Index

About the Author

Jeri Freedman has a B.A. from Harvard University. She has more than fifteen years of experience in sales and marketing for high-tech and medical products companies. She is the author of more than thirty young adult nonfiction books, including *Women in the Workplace: Wages, Respect, and Equal Rights; Being a Leader: Organizing and Inspiring a Group;* and *First Bank Account and First Investments Smarts.*

Photo Credits

Cover (right) © iStockphoto.com/Lukasz Gajdek; cover, p. 1 (top left) © iStockphoto.com/JoKMedia; cover, p. 1 (center left), p. 8 © iStockphoto.com/YinYang; cover, p. 1 (bottom left) © iStockphoto.com/Juanmonino; cover, p. 1 (background) © iStockphoto.com/Dean Turner; pp. 4–5 Fuse/Getty Images; pp. 7, 17, 30, 41 © iStockphoto.com/Don Bayley (detail); p. 9 Joel Saget/AFP/Getty Images; p. 11 Paul Morigi/Getty Images; pp. 14, 18 Justin Sullivan/Getty Images; p. 21 Joe Raedle/Getty Images; p. 23 Jupiterimages/BananaStock/Thinkstock; p. 26 Spencer Platt/Getty Images; p. 29 © iStockphoto.com/Vasiliy Kosyrev; pp. 31, 33, 35 © AP Images; p. 38 © Jeff Greenberg/PhotoEdit; p. 42 Stuart Hughs/Stone/Getty Images; p. 44 © Ian Dagnall/age fotostock/SuperStock; pp. 46–47 Bloomberg/Getty Images; pp. 48–49 Erik Dreyer/Taxi/Getty Images; interior page graphic (arrows) © iStockphoto.com/Che McPherson.

Designer: Sam Zavieh; Editor: Andrea Sclarow Paskoff; Photo Researcher: Marty Levick